Color the Bible™ 3-in-1

Artwork by Michal Sparks
and Lori Siebert

HARVEST HOUSE PUBLISHERS
EUGENE, OREGON

Cover by Katie Brady Design

COLOR THE BIBLE™ 3-IN-1 (VOLUME 2)

Copyright © 2017 Michal Sparks, Lori Siebert
Published by Harvest House Publishers
Eugene, Oregon 97402
www.harvesthousepublishers.com

ISBN 978-0-7369-6965-9 (pbk.)

Printed in the United States of America

16 17 18 19 20 21 22 23 24 25 / VP-JC / 10 9 8 7 6 5 4 3 2 1

A Good Place to Begin

This coloring book is for artists of all ages and talents, and that means you! Let your creative spirit free, choose any color you like, and make each beautiful image your own. There are no rules except to have fun.

Enjoy the process. Feel free to use colored pencils, pens, watercolors, markers, and crayons—or any combination—to add color and texture to each design. Notice that all the pictures are printed on just one side of the paper. To keep colors from bleeding through to the next page, simply slip an extra piece of paper underneath the page you're working on. When finished, you might like to remove the page from the book, trim it to size, and frame your artwork for all to see.

Most importantly, have fun with the process. Enjoy experimenting with contrasting colors or different shades of the same color. Try lighter hues for a softer look, or layer and blend your colors for even more options. Allow some white space or saturate the entire piece with rich, vibrant color, depending on your mood. Let your worries go, relax in the moment, and allow your creative spirit to lead the way!

Color the Psalms

Artwork by Michal Sparks

You will show me
the path of life;
in Your presence is
fullness of joy;
at Your right hand are
pleasures
forevermore.

PSALM 16:11

PSALM 126:3

who lifts up my head. I cried to the LORD with

my voice, and He heard me from His holy hill.

You, O LORD, are a shield for me, my glory and the One

PSALM 3:3-4

The earth is the LORD's,

and all its fullness,
the world and those who
dwell therein.

PSALM 24:1

Psalm 37:3

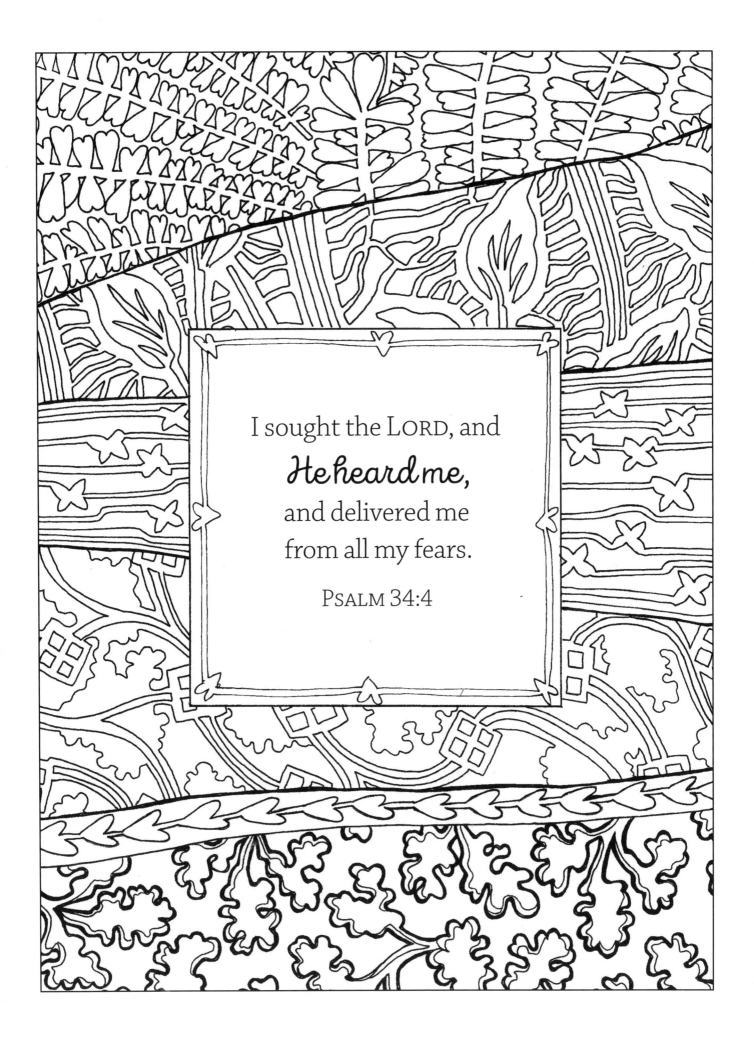

I sought the LORD, and

He heard me,

and delivered me

from all my fears.

PSALM 34:4

Psalm 33:20

The LORD is near to those who have a **broken heart**, and saves such as have a *contrite spirit*.

PSALM 34:18

He hears my voice & my prayer for mercy.

PSALM 116:1

The heavens declare
the glory of God;
and the firmament shows
His handiwork.

PSALM 19:1

the LORD is my shepherd

PSALM 23:1

Our help is in the name of the LORD, who made heaven and earth.

Psalm 124:8

Your word
is a lamp to my feet and
a light to my path.

PSALM 119:105

He alone is my rock and my Salvation.

Psalm 62:2

Restore to me the
joy of Your salvation,
and uphold me by
Your generous Spirit.

PSALM 51:12

The LORD is my light and my Salvation

PSALM 27:1

My cup runs over. Surely goodness and mercy shall follow me all the days of my life; and I will dwell in the house of the LORD forever.

PSALM 23:5-6

Delight yourself
also in the LORD,

and He shall give you
the desires of your heart.

PSALM 37:4

Psalm 46:10

Yea, though I walk
through the valley of
the shadow of death,
I will fear no evil;
for You are with me;
Your rod and Your staff,
they comfort me.

Psalm 23:4

I lift up my eyes to the hills... my help comes from the Lord.

Psalm 121:1-2

I will praise You,
for I am *fearfully* and
wonderfully made;
marvelous are Your works,
and that my soul
knows very well.

Psalm 139:14

Create a pure ♥ in me O GOD

PSALM 51:10

Do not withhold Your tender mercies from me, O LORD; let Your lovingkindness and Your truth continually preserve me.

PSALM 40:11

Teach me to
do Your will,
for You are my God;
Your Spirit is good.
Lead me in the land
of uprightness.

PSALM 143:10

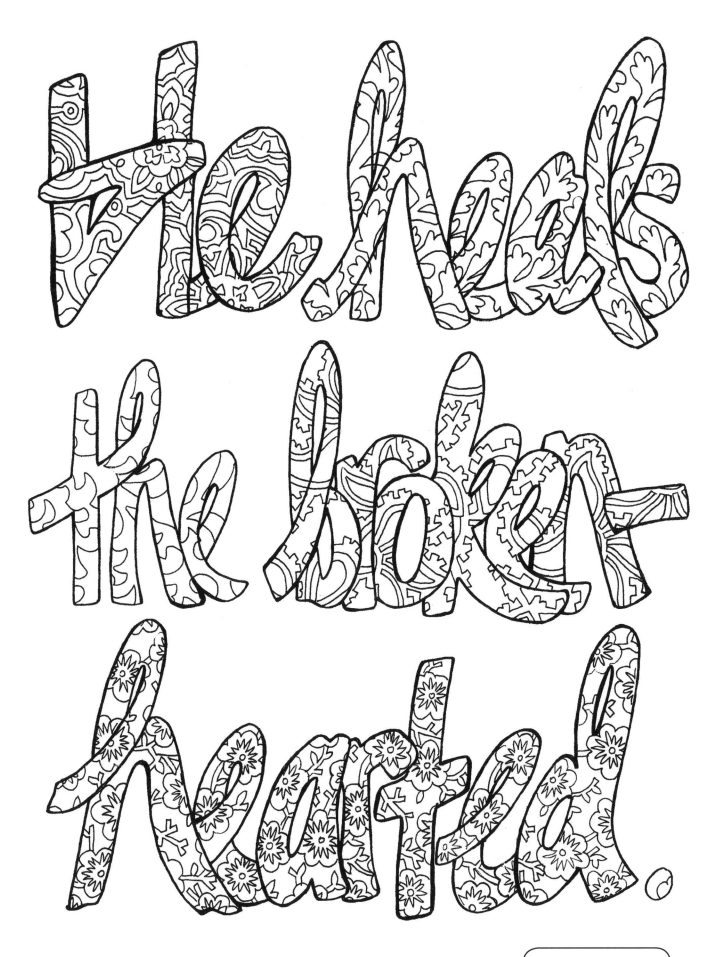

He heals the broken hearted.

PSALM 147:3

Cast your burden
on the LORD, and
He shall sustain you;
He shall never permit
the righteous to be moved.

PSALM 55:22

Psalm 33:20

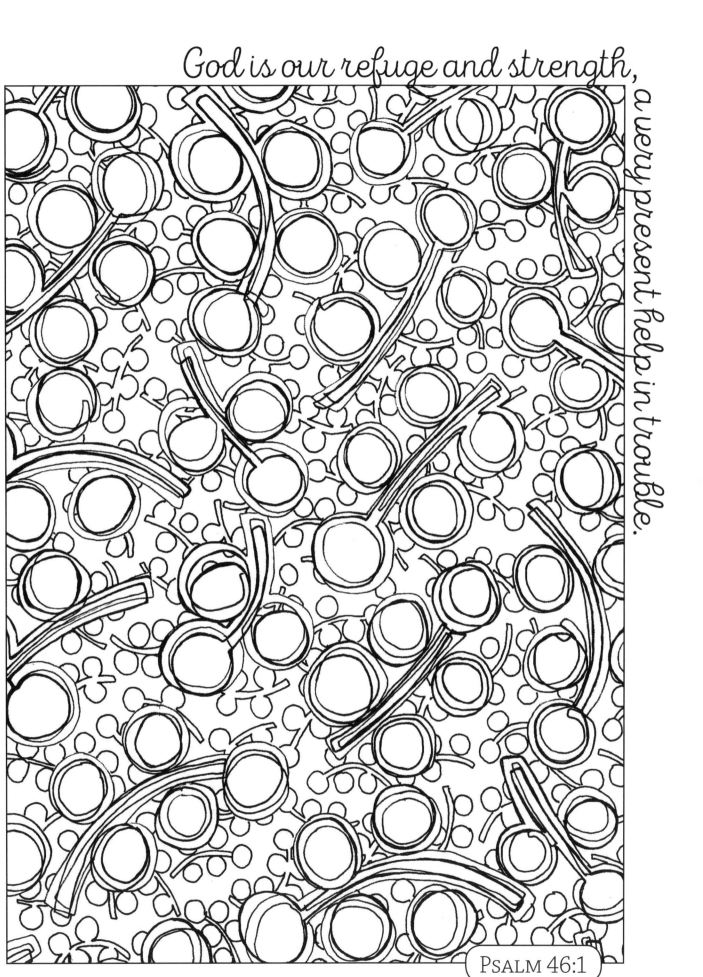

God is our refuge and strength, a very present help in trouble.

Psalm 46:1

When my heart is
overwhelmed;
lead me to the rock
that is higher than I.

PSALM 61:2

Under His wings you shall take refuge.

PSALM 91:4

Give thanks
to the LORD,
for He is good!
For His mercy
endures forever.

PSALM 107:1

His greatness is unsearchable. One generation

shall praise. Your works to another.

Great is the LORD, and greatly to be praised; and

PSALM 145:3-4

This is the day
the LORD has made;
we will rejoice and
be glad in it.

PSALM 118:24

O Lord, my Strength & my Redeemer.

Psalm 19:14

Color the Promises of God

Artwork by Lori Siebert

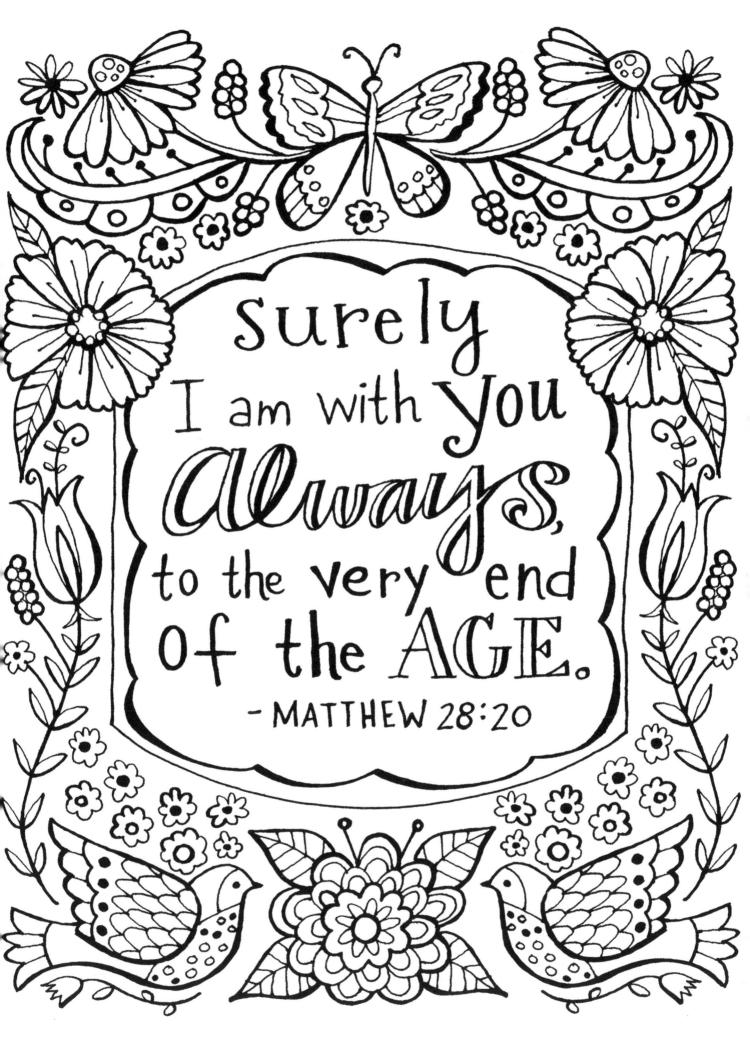

Surely I am with You Always, to the very end of the AGE.

– MATTHEW 28:20

you ARE my HIDING place and my SHIELD.

PSALM 119:114

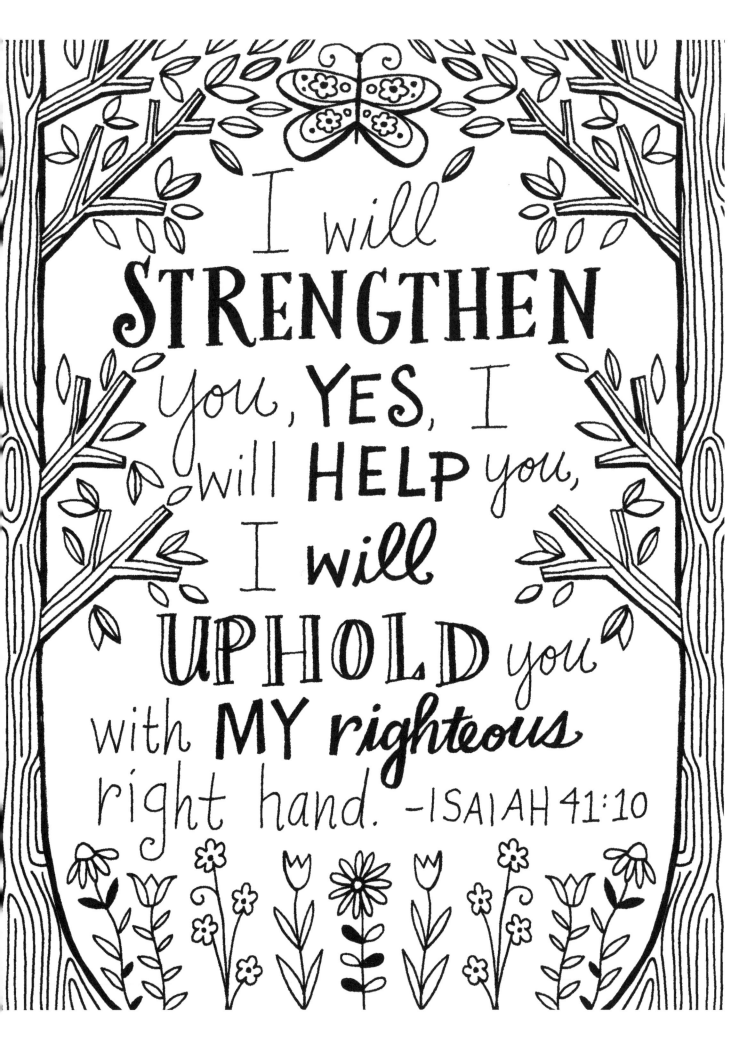

YOU have made the heavens and the EARTH by YOUR great POWER and OUTSTRETCHED ARM. There is NOTHING too hard for YOU.

— JEREMIAH 32:17

GOD is our refuge AND strength, A VERY PRESENT help in trouble. —PSALM 46:1

faith

I will *counsel* you with my *loving* eye on *you.*
—PSALM 32:8

For as in ADAM all die,

so in Christ all will be made ALIVE.

-1 CORINTHIANS 15:22

He ✝ is good... for His lovingkindness is everlasting.
– 1 CHRONICLES 16:34

my GOD will meet all your NEEDS according to the RICHES of his GLORY in Christ Jesus. -Philippians 4:19

Philippians 4:13

I CAN DO ALL things through HIM who STRENGTHENS me.

the LORD will WATCH over your COMING and GOING both NOW and FOREVERMORE.

—PSALM 121:8

If anyone is in **CHRIST**, the *new* *creation* has come: The old has gone, the new is **HERE!**

2 CORINTHIANS 5:17

Blessed are the PURE IN HEART, for they will SEE GOD.

MATTHEW 5:8

the Lord Remembers us AND will BLESS us

-PSALM 115:12

He will COVER You with HIS feathers, and UNDER HIS Wings You will FIND Refuge.

PSALM 91:4

Delight yourself in the LORD and HE will give you the desires of your HEART.
-PSALM 37:4

the **LORD** directs the steps of the **GODLY**. He *delights* in **EVERY DETAIL** of their **LIVES.**

-PSALM 37:23

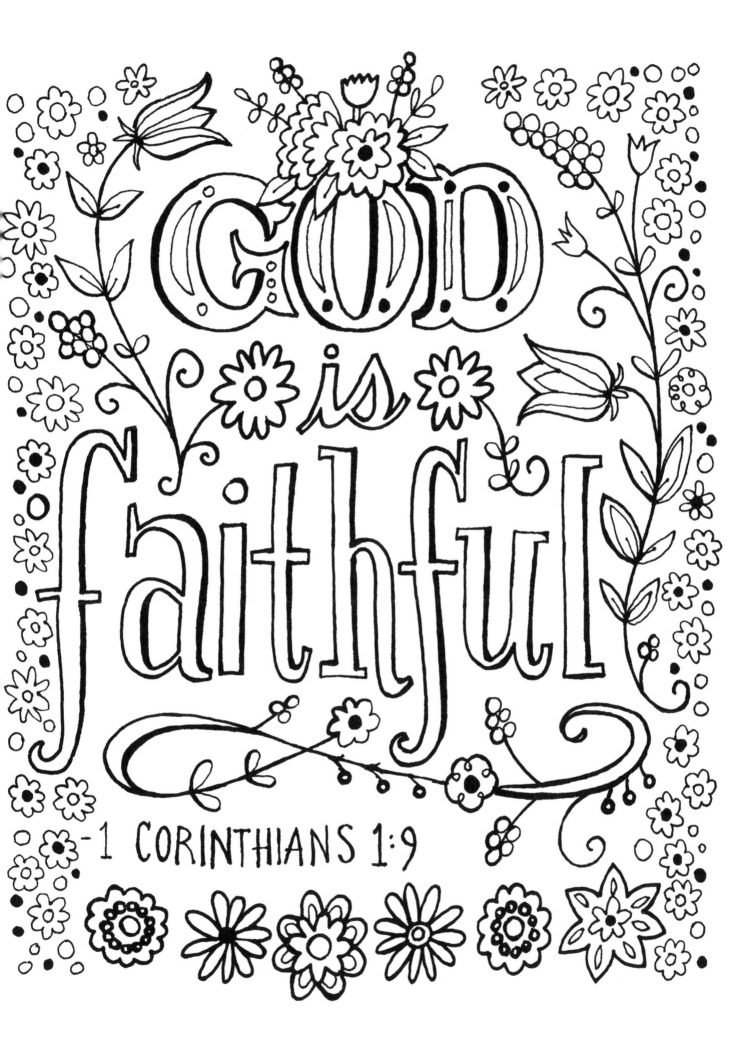

GOD is faithful
-1 CORINTHIANS 1:9

You both **Precede** and **FOLLOW** me and **PLACE** your hand of **BLESSING** on my **HEAD.**

-PSALM 139:5

Color the Proverbs

the

Artwork by Michal Sparks

your neck, write them on the tablet of your heart.

Do not let kindness and truth leave you; bind them around

Proverbs 3:3

A friend loves at all times.

Proverbs 17:17

Above all else,
guard your heart,
for everything you do
flows from it.

PROVERBS 4:23

A person finds joy in giving an apt reply

—and how good is a timely word!

PROVERBS 15:23

A wise man will hear & increase in learning.

Proverbs 1:5

A joyful makes a cheerful face.

PROVERBS 15:13

By *wisdom* the LORD laid
the earth's foundations,
by **understanding** he set
the heavens in place;
by his *knowledge* the watery
depths were divided,
and the clouds let drop the dew.

PROVERBS 3:19-20

Like apples of gold
in settings of silver is
*a word spoken in
right circumstances.*

PROVERBS 25:11

A longing fulfilled is sweet to the soul

PROVERBS 13:19

Trust in the LORD with all your heart and do not lean on your own understanding. In all your ways acknowledge Him, and He will make your paths straight.

PROVERBS 3:5-6

Do not forsake wisdom, and she will protect you;

love her, and she will watch over you.

Proverbs 4:6

Whoever is kind
to the poor
lends to the LORD,

and he will reward them
for what they have done.

PROVERBS 19:17

She is clothed with strength and dignity; she can laugh at the days to come.

PROVERBS 31:25

As water
reflects the face,
so one's life
reflects the heart.

PROVERBS 27:19

A cheerful ♥ is good medicine.

PROVERBS 17:22

The fear of the LORD is a fountain of life

PROVERBS 14:27

Anxiety weighs down the ♥, but A kind word cheers it up.

Proverbs 12:25

As iron sharpens iron,
so one person sharpens another.

Proverbs 27:17

Blessed are those
who find wisdom,
those who gain understanding,
for she is more profitable
than silver and
yields better returns than gold.
She is more precious
than rubies;
nothing you desire can
compare with her.

PROVERBS 3:13-15

Whoever fears the LORD
has a secure fortress,
and for their children
it will be a refuge.

PROVERBS 14:26

The path of the righteous is like the morning sun,

shining ever brighter, till the full light of day.

Proverbs 4:18

Pleasant words are a honeycomb,

sweet to the soul and healing to the bones.

Proverbs 16:24

The fruit of
the righteous
is a tree of life,
and he who
wins souls is wise.

PROVERBS 11:30

PROVERBS 15:1

The fear of the LORD
is the beginning
of wisdom,

and knowledge of the Holy
One is understanding.

PROVERBS 9:10

How much better to get wisdom than gold, to get insight rather than silver!

Proverbs 16:16

A generous
person will prosper;
whoever refreshes others
will be refreshed.

PROVERBS 11:25

For the LORD grants wisdom!
From his mouth come
knowledge and understanding.
He grants a treasure of
common sense to the honest.
He is a shield to those
who walk with integrity.
He guards the paths of the just
and protects those
who are faithful to him.

PROVERBS 2:6-8

Hatred stirs up conflict,
but love covers over all wrongs.

Proverbs 10:12

The name of the LORD is a strong tower; the righteous runs into it and is safe.

PROVERBS 18:10

The mind of man
plans his way,
*but the LORD
directs his steps.*

PROVERBS 16:9

By wisdom
a house is built,
and through understanding
it is established;
through knowledge its
rooms are filled with rare
and beautiful treasures.

PROVERBS 24:3-4

When you lie down,
**you will not
be afraid;**
when you lie down,
your sleep will
be sweet.

PROVERBS 3:24

Commit to the LORD whatever you do,

and he will establish your plans.

Proverbs 16:3

A MAN OF understanding holds his PEACE.

PROVERBS 11:12

Better a little
with the fear of the LORD
than great wealth with turmoil.
Better a small serving of vegetables
with love than a fattened calf
with hatred.

PROVERBS 15:16-17

Michal Sparks' artwork can be found throughout the home-furnishings industry in textiles, gift items, dinnerware, and more. She is the artist for *Words of Comfort for Times of Loss* and *When Someone You Love Has Cancer*. She and her family live in New Jersey.

With an ever-expanding portfolio overflowing with originality, *Lori Siebert* started art lessons at age seven, then earned a degree in graphic design, and now has artwork featured in several books, including *101 Inspirational Thoughts to Brighten Your Day* and *God Cares for You*. She divides her time between sewing, sculpting, drawing, painting, and designing new products.

We'd love to see your creations!
Share your finished projects on social media with the hashtag

#colorthebible

We'll be looking for your artwork!

For information on more
Harvest House coloring books for adults, please visit
www.harvesthousepublishers.com.

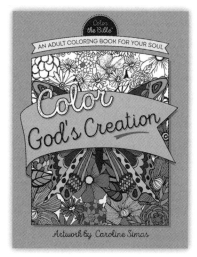

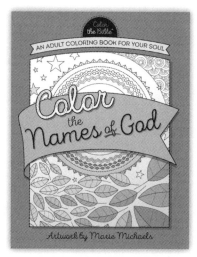